ART OF TH
TRACTOR
COLORING BOOK

OCTANE
PRESS

Octane Press, First Edition
July 2017
© 2017 by Lee Klancher et al.

ISBN: 978-1-937747-83-1

Cover Design by Tom Heffron
Interior Design by Tom Heffron
Project Management by Mary Ham
Copyedit by Chelsey Clammer
Proofread by Leah Noel

On the cover:
Steiger Tiger ST450.
Artist: Santagora

On the back cover:
John Deere 60.
Artist: Todd Cumpston

International 4786.
Artist: Montgomery Design International

On the title page:
International 1456 Turbo.
Artist: Tyler Linner

octanepress.com

CONTENTS

TODD
L
CUMPSTON
2017

J. I. Case Model R

·······························

Artist: Todd Cumpston

From 1936 through 1940, the Case R was in production. The Waukesha four-cylinder gasoline engine delivered 18 horsepower at the drawbar. The styled version was built only in 1939 and 1940.

Todd L. Cumpston—TLC Sketching: A division of ToddCo Industries
info@tlcsketching.com
www.instagram.com/toddpop1
www.toddpop1.tumblr.com

John Deere Model B

....

Artist: Todd Cumpston

The John Deere Model B, introduced in late 1934 as a 1935 model, was a smaller version of the Model A. Produced until 1952, the Model B was styled and redesigned over the years. The Model B came equipped with a 4.25x5.25 bore-and-stroke engine that put out a rated 12 drawbar horsepower and 16 belt horsepower.

Todd L. Cumpston—TLC Sketching: A division of ToddCo Industries
info@tlcsketching.com
www.instagram.com/toddpop1
www.toddpop1.tumblr.com

John Deere Model LA

Artist: Tyler Linner

The John Deere LA was in production from 1941 through 1946. With a two-cylinder gasoline engine delivering 13 horsepower at the drawbar, it was a slightly larger version of John Deere's Model L. The Model LA was among the company's first series of tractors with engine cylinders set vertically and a crankshaft oriented front to back.

www.linnerdesign.com
linnerdesign@gmail.com
www.facebook.com/linnerdesign

J. I. Case Model SC

·······················

Artist: Tyler Linner

Built from 1941 through 1954, the Case SC had a gasoline-fueled, four-cylinder engine delivering 27 horsepower at the drawbar. The SC and the larger DC were the first models built with the Eagle Hitch.

www.linnerdesign.com
linnerdesign@gmail.com
www.facebook.com/linnerdesign

Oliver 66 Orchard

Artist: Panagiotis Gkritzos

The Fleetline Series tractors featured an eight-speed transmission that had six forward speeds and two in reverse. The 66 had a 126-cubic-inch gasoline or diesel four-cylinder engine and was built until 1954.

Pgritzos@hotmail.com

John Deere Model R

....

Artist: Tyler Linner

During the development of the Model R, one of the biggest internal debates that went on was whether to make the tractor with a four-cylinder engine. John Deere's conservative, traditional management decided the engine would be a two-cylinder, despite the considerable engineering challenges inherent in building a large-displacement diesel twin-cylinder engine. About 21,300 Model Rs were created. They were built until 1954.

www.linnerdesign.com
linnerdesign@gmail.com
www.facebook.com/linnerdesign

Orchard 0-2

Artist: Panagiotis Gkritzos

This McCormick 0-2 was custom-built using components from a Farmall A, which began production in 1939. The Farmall A is powered by a four-cylinder gasoline engine that produced 16 horsepower at the drawbar.

Pgritzos@hotmail.com

TODD
L
CUMPSTON
2017

John Deere 60

....

Artist: Todd Cumpston

The John Deere 60 was in production from 1952 through 1956. The two-cylinder engine delivered 37 horsepower at the drawbar when operated on gasoline. This was the first major upgrade of the venerable Model A, which had been built since 1934.

Todd L. Cumpston—TLC Sketching: A division of ToddCo Industries
info@tlcsketching.com
www.instagram.com/toddpop1
www.toddpop1.tumblr.com

Allis-Chalmers WD-45

Artist: Tyler Linner

Introduced in 1953 as the replacement for the WD, the more-powerful WD-45 was available with power steering and Allis-Chalmers' Snap Coupler hitch system. The original WD-45 had a gas engine, and a diesel engine became an available option after 1954. The model was built until 1957.

www.linnerdesign.com
linnerdesign@gmail.com
www.facebook.com/linnerdesign

Oliver Super 55

Artist: Todd Cumpston

The Oliver Super 55 was in production from 1954 through 1958. The four-cylinder gasoline engine delivered 29 horsepower at the drawbar. This was Oliver's first utility tractor.

Todd L. Cumpston—TLC Sketching: A division of ToddCo Industries
info@tlcsketching.com
www.instagram.com/toddpop1
www.toddpop1.tumblr.com

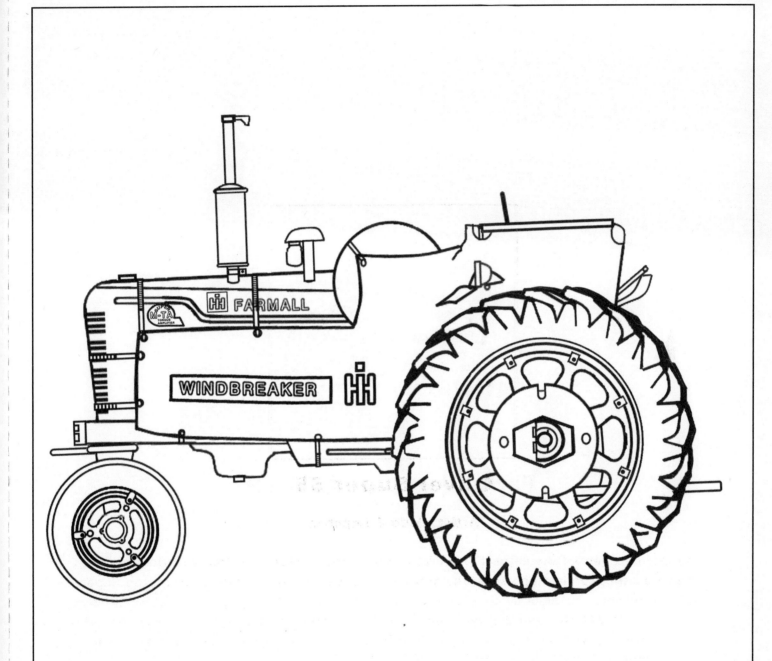

Farmall Super M-TA LP

Artist: Guy Shrum

The last and best of the Letter Series line came in 1954, when International Harvester (IH) rolled out the wonders of a fully independent PTO and torque amplification on the Super M-TA. A planetary gearset allowed the operator to switch speeds on the fly, a feature greatly appreciated when the load bogged the tractor down and a bit of extra power was needed. The tractor was produced at the height of IH's dominance of the tractor market, and nearly 30,000 Super M-TAs rolled out factory doors in 1954.

twostepn2001@yahoo.com

Ford 800 Powermaster

....

Artist: Todd Cumpston

The Ford 800 Powermaster was in production from 1955 through 1957. It had a four-cylinder gasoline engine that delivered 35 drawbar horsepower. It was Ford's first offering of a higher horsepower tractor in an expanded product line.

Todd L. Cumpston—TLC Sketching: A division of ToddCo Industries
info@tlcsketching.com
www.instagram.com/toddpop1
www.toddpop1.tumblr.com

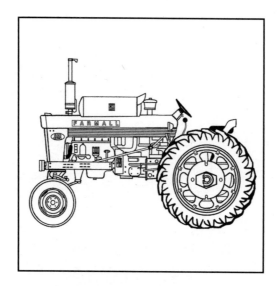

Farmall 560 LP

Artist: Guy Shrum

The 560 is one of the most storied of the 1960 IHC line. Created to meet the growing demand for high-horsepower farm tractors, the 560 came out with a new inline six-cylinder that put out a stout-for-the-time 60 horsepower. The transmission and rear end weren't up to the power, and the tractor faced a recall of epic proportions. The company offered nearly unlimited overtime to employees in order to fix the problem and stories persist to this day of people who bought homes using those overtime paychecks.

twostepn2001@yahoo.com

John Deere 730

Artist: Tyler Linner

This model represents the end of the line for John Deere two-cylinder tractors. This model held the record for diesel tractor fuel economy at the Nebraska Tractor Test Laboratory for 27 years. The 730 was produced from 1958 to 1961, and nearly 25,000 were built. In 1960, the John Deere New Generation series tractors replaced this line.

www.linnerdesign.com
linnerdesign@gmail.com
www.facebook.com/linnerdesign

J. I. Case 730 Orchard

Artist: Tyler Linner

Although the Case 730 was in production for nine years, from 1960 to 1969, the orchard version was fairly rare. This illustration is based on a 1966 LP gas-burning model, originally shipped to Winterhaven, Florida, to be used in the orange groves. The tractor is equipped with a hand clutch, dual-range transmission, and turf tires.

www.linnerdesign.com
linnerdesign@gmail.com
www.facebook.com/linnerdesign

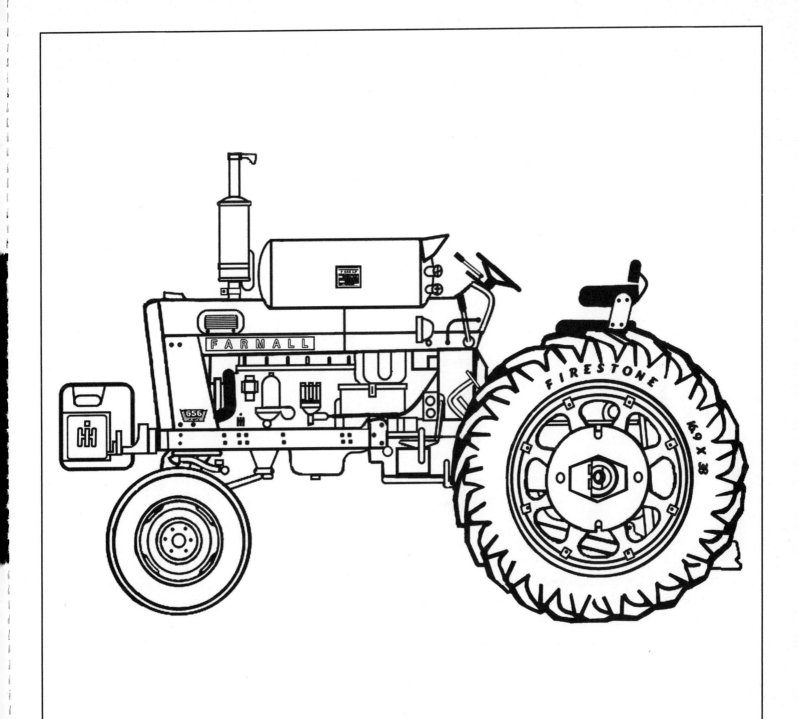

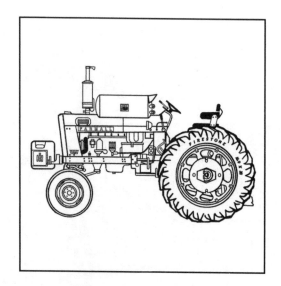

Farmall 656 LP

Artist: Guy Shrum

In its first production year, only Farmall versions of the 656 were available. Customers could order their 656 with one of two available six-cylinder engines. Both the C-263 gasoline and LP engine provided about 64 horsepower at the power takeoff. One could easily identify the tractor with the LP engine by the fuel tank protruding through the hood.

twostepn2001@yahoo.com

International 1456 Turbo

....

Artist: Tyler Linner

For this high-horsepower monster, engineers tuned up the DT-407 engine to produce a shade more than 130 horsepower at the PTO. The tractor also came equipped with a beefier driveline (wider hardened gears, larger bull-pinion and axle shafts, better lubrication, etc.), as well as larger brakes and more engine-cooling capacity. The 1456 was also one of the most fuel-efficient tractors that Harvester produced at the time.

www.linnerdesign.com
linnerdesign@gmail.com
www.facebook.com/linnerdesign

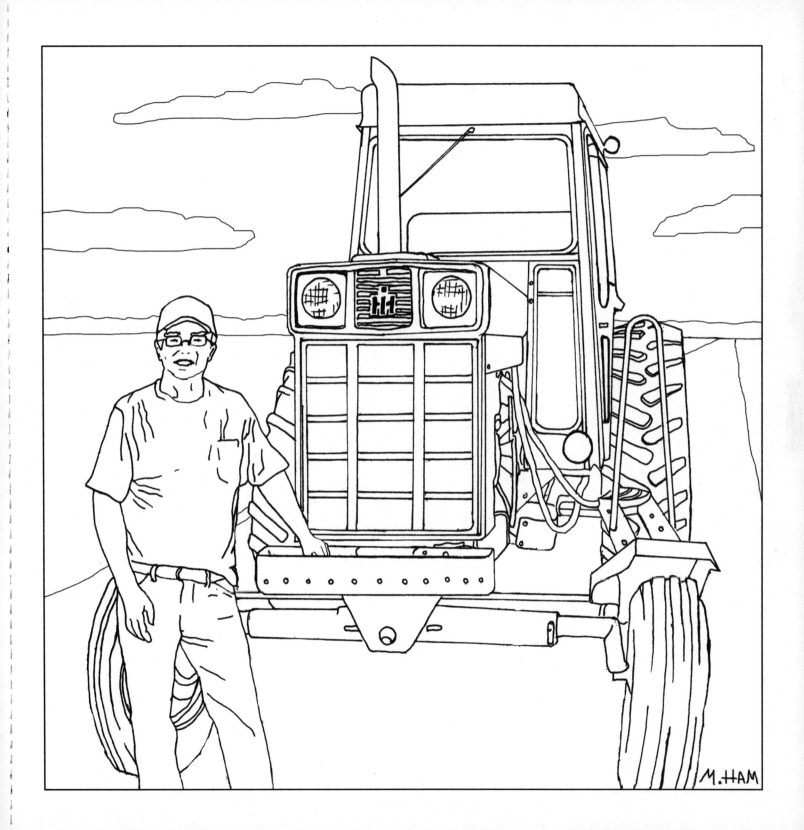

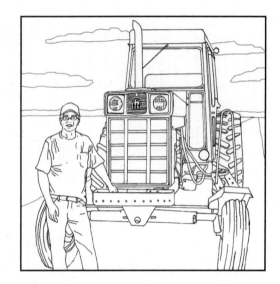

International 1466

....

Artist: Mary Ham

The ISOMOUNT Deluxe Cab on this 1466 reduced vibration and operator fatigue. Its unique, heavily upholstered deluxe cab included a built-in protective frame. The 66 Series used a beefed-up adjustable front axle with less failure-prone spindles, while gauges were brought back to the operator's station. This model could also be ordered with front-wheel drive.

Maryham005@gmail.com

Steiger Tiger ST450

....

Artist: Santagora

The Steiger Tiger ST450 was in production from 1977 through 1982. The Cummins six-cylinder diesel engine provided 369 horsepower at the drawbar. A Caterpillar eight-cylinder diesel engine option produced slightly less horsepower.

www.youtube.com/user/santagora1
www.facebook.com/santagora1

Ford FW-60

....

Artist: Kevin Harger

The Ford FW-60 was in production from 1977 through 1982. This Steiger-built tractor had a Cummins eight-cylinder diesel engine that delivered 271 horsepower at the drawbar. The FW Series tractors were the first articulated four-wheel-drive machines from Ford, and they were built for Ford by Steiger.

www.kevinhargerart.com
kevinhargerart@gmail.com
www.instagram.com/kevinhargerart

International 4786

Artist: Montgomery Design International

The 4786 shared a frame with the other two models in its series (4386 and 4586), and it weighed about 23,600 pounds (1,500 pounds heavier than the 4586). This mighty machine was powered with the DVT-800 V-8 diesel tuned to put out about 350 horsepower at the flywheel, and though there were some engine failures, the V-8 was up to the task. This line was built for IH by Steiger.

www.montgomerydesign.com

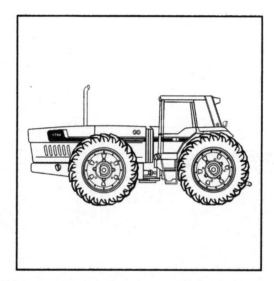

International 3788 2+2

....

Artist: Guy Shrum

This tractor was built on the same principle as the 3388 and the 3588, but its rear section (including the cab) was taken from the 1586—the most powerful member of the 86 Series two-wheel-drive family. With a whopping 170 horsepower available at its 1,000-rpm rear PTO, the 3788 was powered by Harvester's six-cylinder, turbocharged DT-466 Series B diesel engine that was tuned to produce more power than the version installed in the 3588.

twostepn2001@yahoo.com

International 5488

Artist: Tyler Linner

When IH sent each model of the new 50 Series to Nebraska for testing, the 5488 (tested from May 26 to June 8, 1982) set new records for the entire industry to meet. It used fewer pounds of fuel per horsepower hour than any other two-wheel-drive tractor with more than 165 PTO horsepower that was tested at Nebraska. It also recorded 18,646 pounds of drawbar pull, another record.

www.linnerdesign.com
linnerdesign@gmail.com
www.facebook.com/linnerdesign

International 5288

....

Artist: Guy Shrum

Before International Harvester was purchased by Tenneco and became part of Case IH in 1984, the company produced a line of high-tech tractors known as the 30 Series and the 50 Series (along with a very few 70 Series articulated four-wheel drives). The 5288, part of the 50 Series, was powered by a 466-cubic-inch engine rated for 186 PTO horsepower. The 5288 was introduced in 1981 and built until 1984.

twostepn2001@yahoo.com

Teresa Sites

Steiger Panther ST325

....

Artist: Teresa Sites

The Steiger Panther ST325 was in production from 1976 through 1983. The tractor has a Caterpillar 3406 DIT inline six-cylinder engine and provides 20 speeds forward and 4 speeds in reverse when coupled with the 2-speed transfer case.

www.teresasites.com
teresaelizabethsites@yahoo.com

Case IH 4494

Artist: Tyler Linner

In their Racine plant, Case IH built four different models of four-wheel-drive tractors: the 4494, 4694, 4894, and the 4994. The rigid frame allowed four-way selective steering. The 4494 had an advertised 213 gross engine horsepower and a PTO horsepower of 175.

www.linnerdesign.com
linnerdesign@gmail.com
www.facebook.com/linnerdesign

Case IH 7130

Artist: Tyler Linner

The heart of every new 7100 Magnum tractor was the Cummins-built diesel engine. This new engine was compact, strong, quiet, and fuel-efficient. The 7130 had 170 PTO horsepower and the new powershift transmission. The Magnum proved to be one of the most reliable tractors on the market.

www.linnerdesign.com
linnerdesign@gmail.com
www.facebook.com/linnerdesign

Montgomery Design

New Holland TG285

....

Artist: Montgomery Design International

The TG285 was the first model of the second generation New Holland tractors. Nicknamed the "cat's eye" design, this tractor set the styling trend for all modern-day tractors. The unique lighting system was functional as well as stylish, and eclipsed even automobiles for the use of compound lighting. The New Holland line was painted blue, following its Ford heritage.

www.montgomerydesign.com

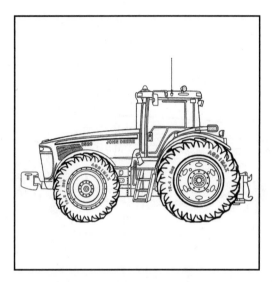

John Deere 8520

Artist: Guy Shrum

The John Deere 8520 was powered by a six-cylinder diesel that delivered 225 horsepower at the drawbar. When the model was introduced in 2002, it was the most powerful row-crop tractor the company had ever produced. The last 8520 model was built in 2005.

twostepn2001@yahoo.com

AGCO Challenger MT975B

....

Artist: Montgomery Design International

Introduced in 2007, the articulated Challenger 4WD tractor was the largest and highest horsepower tractor in the world at that time. In fact, special tires had to be developed to get its massive 500 horsepower to the ground. The MT975B was awarded the International "Good Design" award that same year, and a scale model of the design was on display in Athens, Greece, at the Athenaeum and Museum facility. The tractor is screaming yellow.

www.montgomerydesign.com

Case IH Magnum 275

....

Artist: Montgomery Design International

Introduced in 2006, the third-generation Magnum tractor was one of the best-looking tractors ever produced. Its aggressive styling, attention to fit and finish, and wide horsepower range and features made it the most desirable tractor of its time. It maintains its popularity today.

www.montgomerydesign.com

Case IH Steiger 500

Artist: Tyler Linner

The Case IH Steiger 500 was a part of the new Steiger line for 2011. It used a Selective Catalytic Reduction (SCR) system to meet the Tier 4A emission reduction requirements.

www.linnerdesign.com
linnerdesign@gmail.com
www.facebook.com/linnerdesign

Case IH Magnum 340

Provided by Case IH

This powerful machine is a good representation of all the convenience and high technology offered by modern farm tractors. The 8.7-liter engine is rated for 290 PTO horsepower and mates to a powershift or CVT transmission. Options include autoguidance, HID lighting, CVT transmission, and RowTrac.

Montgomery Design

Asian Concept Tractor

Artist: Montgomery Design International

This sketch is derived from a series of concept designs presented to a large Asian tractor company several years ago. This model must go nameless because it was never manufactured. Proposed to be a 100-horsepower tractor with an upgraded cab and interior, it included modern heating, air conditioning, and communications. This company paints their tractors various colors—so go crazy!

www.montgomerydesign.com

Montgomery Design

STEYR CVT 6225

....

Artist: Montgomery Design International

The Austrian-built STEYR tractor is known for its rugged construction and unique capabilities in mountainous areas. The CVT, which stands for continuously variable transmission, is a unique feature to this model. Its distinctive red-and-white paint visually sets it apart from all other tractors. Many are fitted with both front and rear hitches, and can accommodate nearly any type of field attachment.

www.montgomerydesign.com

Case IH Steiger 600 Quadtrac

Provided by Case IH

The Quadtrac's four-track system was developed at Case IH in the late 1980s and early 1990s. The results were machines that offered class-leading traction and maneuverability for tracked agricultural machines. This 600 was rated for 520 PTO horsepower and weighed more than 30 tons when ballasted with weights for field work.

The Artists

Todd Cumpston is a sketch artist who enjoys exploring handmade forms. His classic cars series is a particular portfolio highlight. Cumpston's other sketches also depict daily human activity, bringing to light moments that are easily lost in our busy world. Working with fountain pen, brush pen, watercolor, and watercolor pencil, Cumpston uses loose, yet simple lines and bright colors to capture forms quickly, yet precisely. Cumpston is available for commission work.

Todd L. Cumpston—TLC Sketching A division of ToddCo Industries
info@tlcsketching.com
www.instagram.com/toddpop1
www.toddpop1.tumblr.com

Panagiotis Gkritzos was born in Athens in 1990 and continues to live there. He studied painting at the Athens School of Fine Arts in a class with Professor Patraskidis Triantafyllos. Gkritzos works with abstraction as he seeks the essence of dreams and mystery in his work—though, line work and discipline sketching are the foundation of his current-day drawing.

Pgritzos@hotmail.com

Mary Ham is a young artist based in Austin, Texas. She graduated from the Western Art Academy at Schreiner University in 2008. Since graduating, Ham has focused most of her artistic energies into portraiture. She loves the challenge of capturing a personality and likeness of an individual.

maryham005@gmail.com

The Artists

Kevin Harger is a freelance artist working in the film industry, currently at Rooster Teeth Productions. His work ranges from loose storyboard sketches to refined, photo-real matte paintings. The fast-paced film industry requires artists to use all sorts of wild techniques to get the point across as quickly and effectively as they can. Harger enjoys the daily challenges he faces at work, along with never knowing exactly what he will be drawing the next day. Focused on improving his art, Harger buys online tutorials and pushes himself to learn techniques he has yet to feel comfortable using.

www.kevinhargerart.com
kevinhargerart@gmail.com
www.instagram.com/kevinhargerart

Tyler Linner is a freelance illustrator and designer based in Flagstaff, Arizona. After obtaining his BFA in Transportation Design from Detroit's College for Creative Studies, Linner worked as a sculptor in the General Motors Design Center for four years. He is currently pursuing a master's degree in Sustainable Communities, with a focus on transportation, at Northern Arizona University.

www.linnerdesign.com
linnerdesign@gmail.com
www.facebook.com/linnerdesign

Montgomery Design International (MDI) is a full-service product design firm located in Westmont, Illinois. Founded in 1983, MDI has arguably become the most prolific consulting design firm in the world focusing on industrial design and styling agricultural and construction equipment. MDI has worked for IH and Case IH since its inception, and for Caterpillar and AGCO for fifteen years. Product lines credited to MDI include the IH 50 Series, the award-winning Case IH Magnum tractors, the New Holland line of "cat's eye" tractors, and the AGCO Challenger 4WD tractor, plus numerous vehicles for other international firms, including Caterpillar, McCormick, Yanmar, JOY, Lovol, and TAFE.

www.montgomerydesign.com

The Artists

Santagora is a young Latvian artist, designer, and vector artist. The main theme in her art is fantasy—from mythological creatures to elven-style-designed tablecloths. Santagora also works as a book illustrator. In 2007, she graduated from the metal design program at Design and Arts Collage at Riga, and then earned both a bachelor's degree and master's degree of multi-visual arts from Art Academy of Latvia.

www.youtube.com/user/santagora1
www.facebook.com/santagora1

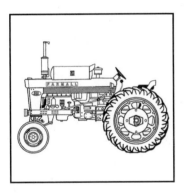

Guy Shrum is a sixty-two-year-old retired truck driver and currently lives in Abilene, Texas. He grew up on a cotton farm near the small town of Ralls, Texas. Shrum's love for tractors started the moment he got his first Hubley toy Ford, and even after all these years that love has yet to lessen. Throughout his life, Shrum has driven and plowed with many different types of tractors and equipment, mostly IH and John Deere, with a Case and an Oliver or two here and there as he helped friends with the harvest. He has always enjoyed drawing and tinkering with computers. And now he has found a way to combine the two: drawing tractors and trucks.

twostepn2001@yahoo.com

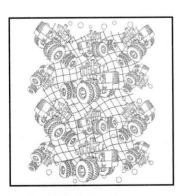

Teresa Sites earned her BA in English and Studio Art from Georgetown University and her MFA in Painting and Drawing from George Washington University. Her artwork explores if everyday surroundings filled with rhythms and repetition suggests that our lives are filled with music. Her artwork has been published several times and is also in private collections, as well as in the collection of the Brooklyn Art Library. Her work was recently featured on *ARTSLANT*'s "Under the Radar."

www.teresasites.com
teresaelizabethsites@yahoo.com

ART OF THE
TRACTOR
COLORING BOOK

If you enjoyed this book, be sure and check out octanepress.com or facebook.com/octanepress for in-depth articles about design and engineering of tractors and motorcycles, as well as high-quality books, calendars and gift cards.

OCTANE
PRESS